W9-AXQ-040

R.A.D.L.
241 East Federal Highway
P.O. Box 888
Roscommon, MI 48653

FAQ

TEEN LIFE™

FREQUENTLY ASKED QUESTIONS ABOUT

Family Violence

Vanessa Lynn
Michaels
and Jeremy Harrow

ROSEN
PUBLISHING®

New York

Published in 2012 by The Rosen Publishing Group, Inc.
29 East 21st Street, New York, NY 10010

First Edition

Library of Congress Cataloging-in-Publication Data

Michaels, Vanessa Lynn.
Frequently asked questions about family violence / Vanessa Lynn Michaels, Jeremy Harrow.
  p. cm.—(FAQ: teen life)
Includes bibliographical references and index.
ISBN 978-1-4488-4628-3 (library binding)
1. Family violence—Juvenile literature. 2. Family violence—United States—Juvenile literature. I. Harrow, Jeremy. II. Title.
HV6626.M526 2012
362.82'92—dc22

2010051936

Manufactured in the United States of America

CPSIA Compliance Information: Batch #S11YA: For further information, contact Rosen Publishing, New York, New York, at 1-800-237-9932.

contents

one

WHAT IS FAMILY VIOLENCE?

Family violence is often the worst kind of violence. It is the ultimate cruelty because it is committed by someone close to you, someone whom you love, respect, or trust. Family violence can occur between spouses, a parent and a child, or any family member with whom you live. These are the people with whom you expect to feel safe but end up becoming the people you fear the most. Whether the abuse is from your parents, another family member, or a legal guardian, it's family violence, and they have no right to do it to you. It's always wrong, and it's illegal. In cases of assault, harassment, incest, or rape, it's a serious crime. You do not have to keep it a secret, and you do not have to keep living with it, even if you're just a witness to it. You have a right to feel safe in your house or in any kind of relationship with the people who are closest to you.

The Reality

In 2003, the U.S. Department of Justice reported that an act of domestic violence occurs at least once a year in 50 percent of all American homes. According to its statistics, family violence represented 11 percent of all violence between 1998 and 2002. If that figure isn't frightening enough, that 11 percent counted for roughly 3.5 million crimes. Half of those cases were committed against a spouse, and the other half consisted of abuse against other family members, such as sons or daughters. More recently, the failing economy has been linked with an increase in domestic violence: a six-week study conducted by the National Domestic Violence Hotline indicated that 54 percent of callers reported a change in their household's financial situation in the past year. If you are in a domestic violence situation, you are not alone.

The Cost of Family Violence

The mental and physical cost to victims is not the only cost of family violence. There is also a significant financial cost for abuse victims.

According to the Texas Council on Family Violence, women who are abused spend 42 percent more on health care each year than women who are not abused. And the increased cost continues even after the abuse ends. Women who had experienced abuse five or more years before continued to pay 19 percent per year more on health care.

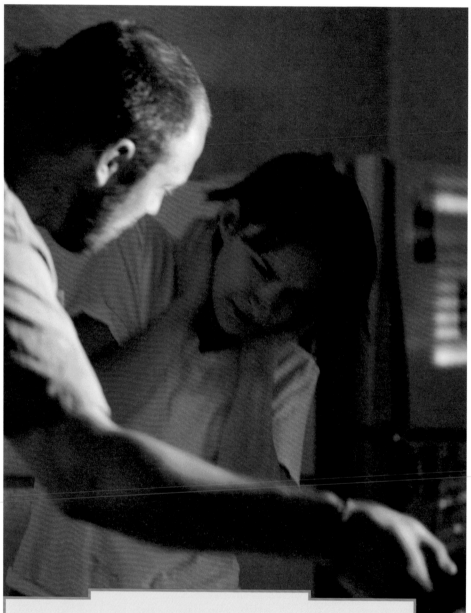

Family violence can occur between parents, siblings, or a parent and child. If someone you know is the victim of family violence, go to a teacher, parent, or school counselor for help.

It Can Happen to Anyone

Domestic violence can happen to anybody. Men, women, and children of all backgrounds can be abused or witness abuse. However, most studies show that women are more often victimized within families than men.

Abuse in relationships often happens to people who have less power and fewer ways to protect themselves, mainly women, and children. However, it is important to realize that women and children are not always the only people being mistreated. Women can abuse men, and children can attack their parents. These cases are rare, but they can and do happen.

People in domestic violence situations are more likely to be abused again than are victims of other types of crime. This behavior is called the cycle of violence. Also, many people who commit these crimes were once abused themselves, usually when they were young. The experience of living with violence is terrifying and harmful. Abused people feel alone and are often ashamed of the abuse. They feel that they are to blame or that they deserve it. They may stay silent because they are afraid of being hurt by their abusers.

Reaching Out for Help

If your parent is abused by your other parent or somebody else, it is important for you to talk to him or her. Ask your parent about the situation and express your feelings. If your parent is unable to make you feel safe, you should go to a school counselor or

Many communities have programs dedicated to fighting and preventing family violence, like this one in Cumberland, Indiana, a suburb of Indianapolis.

other trusted adult to get help. If you are the one being abused, find a good friend or a trusted adult. This is a brave and necessary step.

There are people and many organizations that want to help you, but you need to reach out for the help. You need to make the decision to get out of the dangerous situation. Your call will begin the healing process. It is the only way to break the cycle of family violence.

WHAT ARE THE TYPES OF ABUSE?

Abuse can be physical, emotional, or sexual. The law defines family violence as an act of violence committed by: a spouse or former spouse; someone with whom you have a child in common; an adult person related to you by blood or marriage; an adult person who lives with you or used to live with you; or someone with whom you have a legal parent/child relationship.

Emotional Abuse

Emotional abuse is more difficult to see, but the effects are just as painful. Many people may not even realize they are being emotionally abused. Emotional abuse includes name-calling, insults, blaming, threats, or gestures that cause someone to feel sad, worthless, and degraded.

Abuse can be physical or emotional. Just because an abuser isn't using his or her fists doesn't mean it isn't causing harm to a family member. Verbal abuse can be as harmful as physical abuse.

When parents make their children feel worthless, they are being abusive. Emotional abuse can ruin a person's self-esteem because he or she may grow to believe that the parent's insults are true. A person may not realize that the parent is simply being unreasonable and hurtful. Often the parent may be expressing anger that was caused by something completely unrelated to anything the son or daughter did.

Emotional abuse tears down your self-esteem. The abuser makes you feel worthless. He or she controls you and puts you down through words and threats instead of physical actions.

Emotional abuse is damaging and hurtful. It is just as important to seek counseling and safety for somebody who faces emotional abuse as it is for somebody experiencing physical or sexual abuse.

Verbal Abuse

Verbal abuse is a form of emotional abuse. When someone is using words to hurt your feelings or to belittle you, it is verbal abuse. If your parent or another family member is constantly cursing you out, using profanities to keep you in line, that is no longer normal behavior.

Financial control (control through money) is also a form of emotional abuse. Perhaps the abuser keeps you from getting or keeping a job. Perhaps he or she makes you ask for money, or takes the money that you earn.

Neglect

You might also experience neglect.

If your parents are withholding essentials from you such as food, clean clothing, shelter, medical appointments, mental health care, attention, or affection, that is considered neglect, and it is an especially harsh form of emotional abuse. You have a right to expect those necessities from your parents, and they are required by law to provide them to you.

Physical Abuse

Physical abuse is violent or controlling physical contact that hurts you. It includes pushing, shoving, grabbing, scratching,

Some victims of abuse resort to living on the street, rather than enduring a life of abuse at home. If home life becomes unbearable for you, there are community programs that may be able to help.

hair-pulling, kicking, punching, choking, biting, or slapping. These attacks can result in bruises, welts, cuts, burns, broken bones, or other injuries.

Twisting someone's arm until it causes pain, burning someone, or even extreme tickling are forms of physical abuse. Another form of physical abuse is the use of a weapon, such as a blunt object, a knife, or a gun. Physical abuse will often get much worse over time if the abuser keeps getting away with it. Many unreported cases of physical abuse will eventually result in the abused person's death or homicide. If you are being abused and you don't think your life is in danger now, it very well could be in the future.

Sexual Abuse and Incest

Sexual abuse is unwanted or forced sexual acts, demands, or insults. This includes verbal sexual harassment, unwanted touching, and coerced sex. Sexual abuse can be committed by a stranger, family member, friend, or partner. It is also considered sexual abuse if someone tries to engage in unwanted sexual activity while you are under the influence of drugs or alcohol. The majority of rapes in this country reported to rape crisis centers are by people who know their abuser.

Sexual activity between family members is called incest, and it is a crime if it is between an adult and a minor. No one in your family has a right to be intimate with you. If they tell you it is OK because they are family, they are lying to you. If you are being sexually abused by a family member, go to an adult whom you trust for help. It's difficult, but speaking out and getting help could not only stop the damaging effects on you, but could save someone else from abuse as well.

Statutory Rape

If any adult tries to engage in a sexual relationship with you while you are under your state's legal age for consent (every state varies on what this age is, but it is generally eighteen years old), it is statutory rape and it is a crime. If someone such as an adult friend of the family who is staying at your house tries to tell you that it is OK to have sex with him or her, do not believe that person. It's not.

When the Abuser Is a Woman

Women can be violent, too, whether the abuse is directed at their child or their spouse. Mothers as well as fathers can abuse and neglect children, and they can hurt each other. In fact, some researchers believe that women are just as likely to engage in low-level violence as men. However, they are less likely to engage in severe violence and tend to inflict fewer injuries.

Not all men abuse women; most do not. However, most people who commit crimes of family violence are men or boys. Studies show that the people who become trapped and controlled by violence are usually women and children.

Every day, abuse brings fear and stress to many families. Fortunately there is hope for the people who are abused. There are ways for them to find safety, but this can happen only when the abused are able to recognize the problem.

Volunteers at Teen Lifeline, a crisis hotline, take calls from troubled youths. Programs like this one are there for teens who aren't sure of where to turn.

What Is the Difference Between Discipline and Abuse?

What exactly is the difference between being disciplined and being abused? Sometimes it is tricky to recognize the boundaries between the two.

Discipline is used to correct bad behavior. Being punished when you have gotten into trouble helps teach you what is right and what is wrong.

Being punished when you have not done anything wrong at all is abuse. Your parents do not have the right to discipline you or punish you if it turns into assault. They just cannot cause you any physical injury and justify it as discipline or punishment. However, you may not be able to figure out on your own if your parents have crossed the line from discipline to physical abuse. You will need to talk to a trusted adult outside the family or with someone from a domestic violence organization.

Healthy Relationships

Many teens confuse control with love. Love means trust and support. If your parents are in a healthy relationship, they trust and support each other—even if they do not always agree. In a healthy family, parents will trust and support you. It is hard to know what a healthy relationship is if you have never seen one in your house.

Living with the message that love is violent, you are at risk of becoming violent with your own family members. You have to learn how to have a healthy relationship within your family. A healthy relationship feels good. It allows you to be the person you want to be.

three

WHAT ARE THE WARNING SIGNS?

Abusive behaviors within a family are destructive and dangerous. In many cases they can be life-threatening. The dangers are real. An abuser could be your parent, sibling, spouse, child, or yourself. While there is no stereotypical abuser, many abusers share similar qualities and act in similar ways. Unreasonable anger, yelling, screaming, and insults can be warning signs of abuse. Extreme jealousy, control, and complaints are also danger signals that a situation is not healthy and could become violent.

What Are the Characteristics of an Abuser?

An abuser does not think very highly of himself or herself. He or she feels better when insulting someone else. This is cruel and unhealthy behavior.

Control

An abuser feels better when he or she is in total control. This is not healthy. When one person makes all the decisions, the other is left powerless and dependent on the abuser.

Jealousy

Extreme jealousy and possessiveness are not signs of love. They are signs that the abuser sees you as an object to possess, not a person. An abuser feels that he or she "owns" you.

Most people in a relationship experience jealousy on occasion. But when jealousy turns to violence or extreme possessiveness, it's not normal behavior and you should not take it.

Anger

Watch for these and other clues, such as extreme anger or a short temper. Trust your instincts if you think that you or someone else is in trouble.

Abusers Can Be Anyone

Abusers can be doctors or lawyers, as well as workers in factories or stores. They come from all racial groups. While many abusers have problems with drugs or alcohol, some do not. Most were abused themselves at one time. However, that doesn't mean that if somebody has been through an abusive situation, it is certain that he or she will abuse others later on. There are many people who were abused as children who grow up to become warm and loving adults.

Am I the Victim of Abuse?

In cases of abuse where the abuse is primarily physical or emotional, many victims do not know they are being abused. If you fear you are the victim of abuse, ask yourself these questions:

- Does someone in your family control what you wear, where you go, who you speak to, and how much money you are allowed to spend?
- Do you ever feel like someone in your family is controlling, jealous, or possessive of you? Does he or she need to know where you are at all times?

➤ Does a member of your family insult you or call you names?

➤ Has a member of your family touched you in an inappropriate manner or said things that are inappropriate?

➤ Has a member of your family injured or threatened to injure a family pet?

➤ Does a member of your family ever place blame on you or another member of your family for something that was not your fault?

➤ Has a member of your family broken any objects on purpose or in an attempt to harm you or another member of your family?

➤ Do you ever feel isolated from friends or other relatives because of a member of your family?

If you answered "yes" to any of these questions, you are the victim of abuse. But it is important to remember that you do not have to suffer in silence. See the back of this book about where you can go for help.

four

WHY DOES FAMILY VIOLENCE HAPPEN?

It's hard to say why someone you respect and trust would hurt you, or why your parents would hurt each other. There are no easy answers. Family violence is usually a pattern of controlling behavior. The abuser in a relationship will take complete control over the other person. The abuser will use power to intimidate the abused. He or she may also use control to deal with his or her own uncomfortable feelings. Hurting someone else is the method that the abuser has learned to deal with these feelings.

Sometimes abusers feel out of control themselves, and the only way for them to feel calm and in control is to dominate others. They cannot seem to control their own lives, so they control the members of their families through threats and physical abuse. This is a

Good communication and respect are both signs of a healthy family environment. You should be able to talk to your parent or guardian about things that are going on in your life, good or bad.

destructive way for people to interact. No person should be in control of another. Healthy relationships are about equality and respect, not power and control.

Most parents want their children to do the right thing. Naturally, when a child makes a mistake, the parents might get upset or angry. Those emotions have a clear cause. However, an abuser does not need a reason to be angry or to use violence. When an abuser becomes violent, that person may be upset about something in his or her own life. He or she could be having other problems, be feeling out of control, or be displacing his or her anger on the child. Abusers have trouble managing their anger and will often release it through violence.

What Causes Abuse?

When people resort to violence, it is usually because they think it will help them get something that they want. Some abusers use violence because they do not know how to get what they want any other way. A single mother may turn to her child with needs that can only be met by another adult. When the child cannot meet these needs, the mother becomes abusive. A man may want to be comforted, but he may not know how to ask his wife to comfort him. He blames her for his failure and becomes violent. Abuse can be triggered by many different things:

- Unrealistic expectations. A parent may expect a child to be able to do impossible things. He or she may want the child to be perfect, even though no child is perfect. That is an unrealistic expectation. When the child fails to live up to unrealistic expectations, the parent may lose control and abuse the child.
- Stress. When a parent is under extreme stress from problems at work, with family, or with friends, he or she may become very angry at the world in general. The parent may take out his or her anger and resentment on the family through abuse.
- A history of abuse. Many abusers were themselves abused as children. Because they grew up with violent

Even if family violence is not affecting someone directly, it nevertheless can create stress and strain if it goes on for a long period of time.

role models, they learned to deal with emotions through violence. With a family of their own, they may repeat the actions of their early abusers.

➤ Drug abuse or mental illness. Any kind of drug, from alcohol to cocaine, causes personality changes in the user. While under the influence of the drug, he or she may lose control and become unable to handle problems rationally. The same is true of those suffering from mental illness. Because they are emotionally unstable, they may express themselves through abuse.

A Learned Behavior?

An abuser has usually seen violence in his or her own family. He or she never learned how to interact and establish a healthy relationship. Abused children grow up learning that it's OK to hurt other people or let other people hurt them. In future relationships, they will turn to the familiar method of interaction: violence. This is how a person who has endured domestic violence can turn into an abuser.

The Pattern of Abuse

Violence is not a one-time act. It is a cycle, a pattern. An abuser will create a pattern of behavior in his or her relationship. There will be good times, and there will be bad times. The good times are often called the "honeymoon phase." These usually follow an episode of violence. During the honeymoon phase, the abuser may seem very caring and sensitive. He or she will try and make up for the abuse, and perhaps even apologize for it. The worse the abuse is, the sweeter this phase will be. People who are abused often stay in their relationships because they are waiting—and hoping—for the next good time. However, it is important to understand that abuse is a learned behavior. It is a belief system, and only the abuser can change his or her behavior with hard work and professional help. You can't change his or her behavior.

Why Do People Stay with Someone Who Is Abusing Them?

It can be difficult to understand why people would continue to live with someone who hurts or threatens them. There are

If you are a victim of any type of abuse, it's important to remember that you are never alone. Many communities have group therapy programs for abuse victims.

several reasons that people who are abused typically give for remaining in an abusive relationship:

➤ They blame themselves for the abuse. An abuser may have made the abused feel that he or she deserves the violence.

➤ The abusers have threatened them. Those who are abused may be afraid that violent family members will hurt them if they try to leave.

➤ They think that the violence is normal or acceptable. This may be true for people who were raised in a violent home or believe that a husband is permitted to hurt his wife.

- They are too ashamed to admit that there is a problem. They may try to keep others from knowing about the violence by pretending that it is not happening.
- Abused people are afraid that no one else will love them. They may stay with abusive spouses because they are afraid of being alone.

In all of these situations, the abused person feels too afraid to confront the problem and get help. To survive family violence, abused people must overcome the emotions that keep them from recovering. Crisis counselors at mental health centers and shelters for battered individuals can talk with people who have been abused about their fears and help them find safe solutions.

What Is the Abuse Cycle?

Even though the abuser will often feel ashamed or guilty about the abuse, he or she will refuse to take responsibility for his or her actions. The abuser may blame the person he or she is abusing for provoking the abuse, try to justify it, or deny it. This is wrong. Remember, the person who is abused is never at fault when violence or abuse occurs. You may be vulnerable and needy, but nobody wants or deserves to be hurt.

It is important to remember that the problem is with the abuser. You cannot change an abuser. He or she must seek professional help. You do not have control over the violence in your house. You do, however, have a choice about how to respond.

You can break the cycle by getting yourself into a safe situation where you are treated with the respect that you deserve.

Inexcusable Behavior

Whatever the excuse somebody has for being abusive, that doesn't mean it's OK. Jealousy, financial pressure, alcohol or drugs, depression, and other types of mental illness are the most common excuses given. An abuser may tell you that he or she had a bad day or too much to drink. An abuser may tell you that you deserved to be hit because you are "stupid" or something similar.

These are just excuses and are unacceptable. They are not true, and they are unfair. There is no excuse for abuse. The only way to stop abuse is to recognize what abuse is. Treating yourself and others with respect is a choice you make, no matter what situation you were raised in.

It's Not Your Fault

If you or a member of your family is suffering due to any type of abuse by another family member, remember that what's happening is not your fault. There was nothing you did to cause it, and there may be nothing you can personally do to resolve it. Sometimes it takes someone of authority stepping in on your behalf. Feelings of guilt are the result of being in an abusive environment. If it helps, you may even want to repeat "It's not my fault" to yourself as a reminder.

Myths and Facts

Domestic violence does not affect that many people. Fact ➡ A 1998 National Crime Victimization Survey found that one million violent crimes were committed against people by their current or former spouses, boyfriends, or girlfriends.

Emotional or verbal abuse is not as bad as physical abuse. Fact ➡ Emotional or verbal abuse can do just as much damage as physical abuse. Hurtful words and constant put-downs can leave deep, psychological scars that may never fully heal.

As long as it's just slapping and pushing, it will never get worse. Fact ➡ Slapping and pushing can easily escalate into punching and choking. Abuse usually worsens over time. Physical abuse can become deadly if the person decides to use a gun, a knife, or a blunt object like a baseball bat.

I must have done something wrong to be abused.

Fact ➡ There is no excuse for anyone to ever abuse you. No one has the right to hurt you, not even your parents.

What goes on in my family is nobody else's business.

Fact ➡ If a family member is physically or sexually abusing you or anyone else, he or she is committing a serious crime and can be arrested for it. He or she wants to keep the abuse secret, and an abuser has no right to privacy. You do not have to keep it a secret.

HOW DO I BREAK THE CYCLE OF ABUSE?

Abuse can come in many forms. Even though every situation is different, your instincts will tell you when something is wrong. It won't feel right. A "red flag" (warning sign) will rise when someone hits or insults you.

When somebody crosses your boundary, listen to your internal warning signal. This is your personal security alarm. If a situation feels wrong, get out! No matter what the other person says to you, always trust your instinct. Only you can know what feels wrong, and only you can do something to change it.

Where to Go for Help

Although it is normal to feel alone, reaching out for help is the beginning of the healing process. The first step is to

Seeking the help of a trusted adult can be a very difficult thing to do, but sometimes it is necessary in order to get an individual out of an unhealthy environment.

tell someone you trust, a close friend or a trusted relative, about the abuse. If you feel you cannot tell a parent, tell another adult you trust—a teacher, doctor, or friend's parent. Remember that when you tell an adult, in many cases that adult is required to report the abuse to child protective services. Telling someone is the first step to getting out of the situation.

Healing is a journey. It starts with a question: "What can I do?" There are many different answers. Ultimately, the choice is up to you. You need to make the choice that will help you become a happier, healthier person living in a safe environment.

Living with Abuse

If you cannot get yourself out of an abusive situation, there are things you can do to protect yourself from injury. If you sense an oncoming attack, try to be near a door to the outside or a door you can lock from the inside. Do not stand near an open window. Try to protect your face, chest, and abdomen from assault. Do not reason with your abuser or try to hit back. In most cases, the attacker will only become angrier. Do what you can to save yourself.

Create a code word that you can give to a trusted adult. If you need to call him or her for help, you can use this code word. It will signal that you are in trouble, but it won't alert the abuser.

If you can, call the police. In some states, the police can remove the abuser from the home on a temporary basis, even if you do not press charges against him or her. This is called temporary protection. If the attack is serious, the police can make an arrest. They can also take you to a shelter (although most shelters will not take teenagers without a guardian), or to the home of a trusted adult. They will help you receive medical treatment and provide you with helpful information on your legal rights.

Collect Evidence

If you receive medical help, don't be afraid to tell the doctor that you have been abused. He or she will know to keep a record of your injuries and collect evidence for the police. Ask the doctor

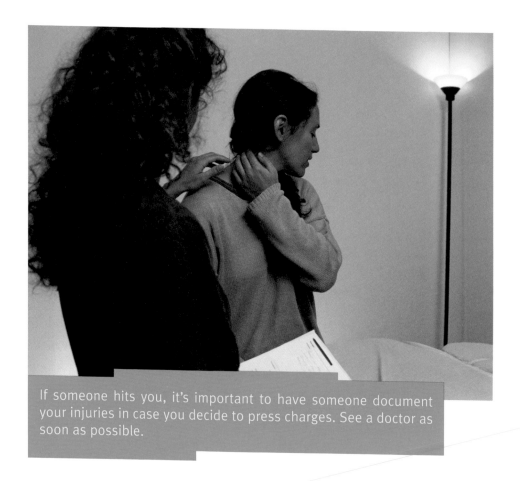

If someone hits you, it's important to have someone document your injuries in case you decide to press charges. See a doctor as soon as possible.

or nurse to take pictures of your injuries. These photographs can be used later as evidence if you decide you want court protection. Save torn clothing and broken or damaged objects—anything that can be used to show evidence of abuse.

Domestic violence does not go away on its own. You will have to take action if you want the abuse to stop. Remember, domestic violence is a crime, and you do not have to tolerate it. You have the right to live a healthy, successful life.

Report Your Parents

Everyone looks to his or her parents for love and attention. It is a natural reaction to have mixed feelings about your abusive parent. You might feel sorry for your mother and want to help her because she was abused as a child. At the same time, you might feel angry that she continues to abuse you just as she was abused. Maybe you are waiting for the love and attention she gives to you during the good times. Or maybe you are afraid that if your mother is taken away, your father will be alone.

In most states, the goal of the legal system is to protect the abused, not to punish the abusive parent. In some cases, the social worker will try to get help for your parent through counseling and/or support groups. In those cases where the danger is more serious or life-threatening, the courts will take the necessary action to keep you safe and punish the abuser.

If you are being physically or sexually abused by one of your parents, your rights as a minor (a person under the age of eighteen) are complicated. In most states when you tell any adult—a school official, a doctor, a nurse, a therapist, a police officer, or a domestic violence advocate—that you are being abused, he or she is considered a mandated reporter. He or she is required by law to report the abuse to the child protective services in your area. The child protective agency will open an investigation once the abuse has been reported. You will be interviewed, as will your parents and anyone else involved in the situation. During the investigation, the child protective agency may decide that it is necessary that you live outside the home. This is for your own safety. You will be asked to stay with a trusted adult or a family member. Although all of this will be difficult, it is a necessary process to end the abuse.

Alternatives to Filing a Report

If you do not want to report your abuse, you can call a domestic violence agency and ask for help anonymously. Most advocates will answer your questions even if you do not want to give your name. Being underage means that you probably don't have enough money to survive on your own. But you may know a trusted adult with whom you would be willing to live until your home feels safe again or until you can start your own life.

You Can Help a Parent

If one of your family members, such as a parent, is being abused, you need to help your loved one by being supportive and helping him or her get out of the situation. Although this situation might be especially difficult to deal with and you may feel that you are putting your own safety at risk or jeopardizing your relationship with the person who is doing the abuse, remember that your loved one is suffering and often doesn't know how to help himself or herself. You may have a chance to stop the abuse by telling someone or by helping get your loved one out of the abusive household and to a safe place. This is a heavy task. You may need to seek the help of another adult, a counselor, or a professional at a domestic violence organization.

This domestic violence intake specialist talks to female abuse victims about obtaining a restraining order against their abusers before they go before the judge.

You Can Help a Friend

If you think your friend is being hurt, you may feel helpless. It is difficult to know what to say. You may feel awkward or uneasy about interfering in someone else's family, but abuse is everybody's business. Your friend's health and welfare are in danger because the abuse will not stop. It will only get worse.

If a friend confides in you that he or she is being abused by a family member, there are many things you can do to help. Listening is the most important. Be sympathetic and careful not to blame or embarrass him or her. Encourage your friend to talk to a trusted adult—offer to go along if he or she needs your support. Let your friend know that the violence is the abuser's fault, not his or her fault.

The most important thing is to make sure that he or she is safe. Work with your friend to make a plan to protect himself or herself. If the situation becomes life-threatening, help your friend get to a safe place.

There are many different organizations that provide help to people facing domestic violence. These include shelters, mental health centers, hospitals, private therapists, churches, temples, and social service organizations for youth, such as Covenant House.

Do not be discouraged if your friend does not immediately agree to seek help. Be patient with your friend, and do not give up. It is often hard for someone to accept that he or she is being abused. Remember that the love and support you give your friend may be the only love and support he or she has in life.

10 Great Questions to Ask Your School Counselor or Therapist

1 Can I live with my other relatives if I don't feel safe in my parents' house?

2 Will my teachers understand if I can't concentrate on my schoolwork because of the problems I'm having at home?

3 When is the right time to get the police involved?

4 Which is the best organization for me to contact to help me with my problem?

5 Is staying at home and living with abuse better than running away and trying to live on my own?

6 Is there any way to stop the problem without getting other people involved?

7 Is it OK to use alcohol or drugs to deal with the pain?

8 If I do nothing to stop what's going on at my house, am I just as guilty?

9 Is it OK to fight back physically when someone is trying to abuse me?

10 Will I end up abusing someone one day because I've been abused?

WHAT ARE MY RIGHTS?

Family violence is against the law. But the law—and how it will apply to you as somebody in a domestic violence situation—differs from state to state. Even the definition of a domestic relationship varies from state to state. Many advocate groups are trying to establish laws that would recognize emotional abuse as a crime punishable by law.

Every state has two sets of laws: criminal and civil. Under the criminal laws in most states, physical and sexual abuse, or the threat of this kind of abuse, is a crime. The abuser can be tried and punished as a criminal.

Criminal Charges

If you would like to press criminal charges against the abuser, you can call the police and report him or her. The

If you decide to take legal action against a family member for abuse, a police officer can help you press charges and keep you safe from harm.

police will then write up a report of the abuse. A written report is required by law. Be sure to insist that it is in fact written down. If your abuser is arrested for or charged with a crime, you have the right to ask the police to obtain a "no contact order," also known as a restraining order. This prevents the abuser from having any contact with you.

If your abuse case goes to criminal court, you will be represented by an attorney for the state in which you live. This person will prosecute the crime (the physical or sexual violence). This attorney is usually known as the prosecutor, county attorney, or district attorney.

Civil Law

No matter what your relationship is to your abuser, you have rights. You have the right to expect help and protection. Cases of domestic violence under civil law are handled in family court. In family court, the abuse is not looked at as a crime. It is looked at as a violation of your rights as a private citizen. It is important to remember that the laws will differ for different types of relationships (i.e., parent/child, husband/wife).

In civil court (family court), a guardian may be required to act in your best interests. The civil court will also appoint a lawyer to represent you free of charge.

How You Can Take Legal Action

In most states, you can pursue your case in both criminal and civil court. It depends on your needs and goals. You might want

A family court judge signs court orders for people dealing with family violence. Going before a court can be a frightening experience, but the judge is there to help you.

to go to civil court while also seeking relief from the abuse through the criminal courts with an order of protection. You might ask to be removed from your home—though that decision will ultimately be made by a family court judge.

Many states have a crime victims agency that can offer you assistance. It will answer your legal questions and work with you and your family to understand your rights. In other states, a domestic violence advocate will help you file orders, accompany you in court, and answer your legal questions.

What Is an Order of Protection?

If you do not want to press criminal charges but do want to protect yourself, you can request an order of protection. This sets limits on the behavior of the abuser. He or she will no longer be able to threaten or hurt you. If he or she breaks this order, the courts will punish him or her.

Custody

An order of protection may also take custody away from the abusive parent and allow him or her only supervised visits with you. The supervision can be provided by the other parent, a social worker, or a trusted adult friend.

In most cases, the abusive parent can no longer live in the same place as you. He or she must leave your home, or arrange to have you stay with a guardian. If both parents are abusive, the court may place you in a foster home.

Emancipation

You can also ask the court for emancipation. This means the court considers you to be an adult and thus allows you to live on your own. For this to happen, there are often age requirements.

When It's Emotional Abuse

Emotional abuse is not yet considered a crime. However, emotional abuse is still extremely destructive. You have a right to seek help and get relief.

A domestic violence counselor talks to a victim about her options for keeping herself and her children safe. Making the decision to leave an abusive home is a hard one.

Domestic violence agencies will help you answer questions about your relationship. They will offer suggestions to help you find a way out of the emotional abuse. Many domestic violence agencies also offer support groups. Some of these groups are aimed at teenagers like you. Most schools offer the services of a trained therapist or psychologist who can help you sort out your feelings and regain your self-esteem.

Making Your Own Decision

You have the choice to press charges against the abuser. You may decide to leave the abuser and seek help. If your life is in danger, you need to get out of the situation for good. The abuse will not stop unless the situation is changed.

seven

HOW DO
I SURVIVE
THE ABUSE?

Domestic violence can happen to anyone. Even if you came from a home where there was no abuse, an abusive partner can still pull you into his or her cycle of violence. You may not realize right away that you are in an abusive relationship.

Everybody wants to be loved. When someone pays attention to you—a parent or a sibling—it feels good. Maybe you think that the abuser has changed. He or she may compliment you or buy you things. The abuse rarely starts immediately. When it does start, it will not stop without some form of intervention.

Healthy relationships have conflicts, too. While these conflicts can lead to arguments, in a healthy relationship no one person is in complete control. Problems are solved with discussion and understanding, not with violence and insults.

Once you escape from an abusive environment, it can take a while before you are able to feel completely safe. A therapist or counselor can help you make the adjustment.

Abuse Survival

It is difficult to have an exact number of how many people face domestic violence because many are afraid to report the abuse and instead find ways to disguise it. Some invent stories about their injuries. Others deny it. Many abused people get family members, friends, teachers, and even doctors to believe their stories. They may be ashamed to admit the abuse. They often feel trapped, alone, and scared. Some people try to survive in their situations by isolating themselves from friends and family. They are afraid to trust anybody. This is a way of protecting themselves from more pain.

People who are abused will often think of their abuser as two people: the person who compliments them and the person who tells them that they are worthless. When you separate the abuser from the harm that he or she causes, it becomes easier to focus on the good that he or she does. You try to forget the cruel side of the person.

Staying in an abusive situation is dangerous. You need to reach out for help. Find a trusted adult friend or family member who can help protect you. Explain the situation and express your feelings and fears. He or she will help you learn how to feel good and believe in yourself again, and support you when you are ready to get help.

Where to Go

When you live with violence, either at home or in a dating rela-tionship, drugs and alcohol may seem attractive. They appear to offer an escape from your nightmare. This is false. After the high wears off, your problems are still waiting for you.

You may feel like running away from home, dropping out of school, or dropping out of life. These are all normal feelings. When you are abused, you lose your strength, hope, and self-respect. You may feel depressed and trapped. It may seem that there is no way out.

Some people who are abused deal with their feelings by hurting others. This is how the cycle of violence continues. Dropping out, running away, and doing drugs are only tempo-rary escapes for your anger. They will not make your feelings of pain or depression go away; they will only make them worse.

You Can Ask for Help

The best way to stop the pain is to get out of the situation. While you cannot force the abuser to get help, you can get help for yourself. There is counseling available to help you deal with your emotions in a healthy way. But before anyone can help you, you need to let people know that you are being abused. You need to ask for help.

The Future

It is important that you remember that it's not your fault. If you are in a violent relationship, you do not have to suffer in silence. Reach out to an adult that you trust for help. Your situation may be too dangerous for you to seek help. In this case, your first pri-ority is to get yourself out of the situation immediately.

If you discover that a friend is the victim of family violence, you can do a number of things to help, including going to a trusted adult or simply giving your friend someone to talk to.

Building a new life takes time. Many states have support groups for teenagers who are being abused. Talking to other teens about your experience will make you feel less alone. Their stories will be familiar to you, and yours will be to them. You can bring the things you have learned about your relationship to others. These meetings can give you a safe space to explore your feelings. You can bring up your questions and your fears. You will not be judged, and you will get information.

Seeking the help of a therapist or family counselor can be a valuable asset to your recovery once you are removed from an abusive environment. At first it can be difficult to talk about what you've experienced, but after some time and realizing that you are not alone, sharing becomes a lot easier.

Once you are safe, it is important to feel good about yourself again. You are a valuable person. You will need to teach yourself new ways of forming relationships. You will need to learn new ways to deal with people. Increasing your independence is an important first step.

Independence

The more independent you are, the better your chance of breaking the cycle of abuse and moving on with your life. You need to know that you are a responsible, intelligent person. You need to know that you can take care of yourself. It is OK to look to others for support and love, but you need to respect yourself and know that you are strong. Here are some ways to increase your independence:

- Learn the public transportation routes near your home. Knowing these routes allows you your own mode of transportation. You can find bus, subway, or train routes for your area online.
- Find ways to get yourself to and from appointments, school, and work. If you are not old enough to drive yourself, seek out a trusted adult for assistance.
- Learn the names and numbers of a trusted adult, doctor, social worker, and your landlord. Record these and other important numbers in your address book or cell phone.

➤ Get a part-time job so that you can earn your own money. A good place to start looking is your local newspaper or online. And keep an eye out for job opportunities at stores or restaurants that you visit on occasion.

➤ If possible, open your own bank account and learn how it works to keep track of your own finances. This will be a great benefit to you when you are an adult and must take full responsibility for your bills and expenses.

These steps are not easy. It will take time to learn what good emotional health is supposed to feel like and to learn how to trust other people again. But take the time—it is worth it because your physical and mental health are important. Being with caring people who support you, value you, and respect you is something you deserve. You cannot change the abuser, but you can work on yourself. By regaining control of your life and getting help, you can break the cycle of domestic violence.

abuse The mistreatment of one person by another.

advocate A person who works to support and argue on behalf of another.

assault A violent physical attack.

coerce To force someone to do something.

consent Permission to do something.

cycle of violence When someone who was abused as a child continues the pattern of abuse on his or her children or spouse.

emotional abuse Name-calling, insults, blaming, threats, or gestures that cause someone to feel sad, worthless, and degraded.

guardian A person legally in charge of the affairs of a minor to protect his or her best interests.

harassment The act of tormenting another person with persistent threats, insults, or unwanted attention.

incest Sexual intercourse between two closely related people.

intimidate To make someone afraid, as with threats of violence.

jealousy A feeling of envy or suspicion toward another person.

mental illness The psychological state of having emotional or behavioral problems serious enough to require psychiatric intervention or medication.

minor Someone who is not yet a legal adult.

neglect The lack of proper care, or denial of affection or attention.

no contact order A court order that prevents one person from having any contact with another; also known as a restraining order.

order of protection A document issued by a court to help protect a person from harassment or abuse.

physical abuse When one person attacks another person with hands, feet, an object, or a weapon.

profanity Obscene or vulgar language; more commonly known as curse words or dirty words.

self-esteem How one feels about himself or herself.

sexual abuse Any unwanted sexual activity that is forced upon another person.

sexual harassment The making of unwanted and offensive sexual advances or sexually offensive remarks or acts by one person to another.

spouse A husband or wife.

statutory rape Sexual intercourse between an adult and someone who is younger than the age of consent as defined by law.

Assaulted Women's Helpline
P.O. Box 369 Station B
Toronto, ON M5T 2W2
Canada
(866) 863-0511
Web site: http://www.awhl.org
The helpline is available twenty-four hours a day, seven
    days a week.

Break the Cycle
5200 W. Century Boulevard, Suite 300
Los Angeles, CA 90045
(888) 988-TEEN (8336)
Web site: http://www.breakthecycle.org
Break the Cycle is a nonprofit organization whose mission
    is to engage, educate, and empower youth to build
    lives and communities free from dating and domestic
    violence.

Canadian National Clearinghouse on Family Violence (NCFV)
Family Violence Prevention Unit
Public Health Agency of Canada
200 Eglantine Drive
Ottawa, ON I9O 9D1

Canada

(613) 957-2938

Web site: http://www.hc-sc.gc.ca/hppb/familyviolence

The NCFV provides information on violence within relationships of trust.

Family Violence Prevention Fund

383 Rhode Island Street, Suite #304

San Francisco, CA 94103-5133

(800) 595-4889

Web site: http://www.endabuse.org

The Family Violence Prevention Fund works to prevent violence within the home and in the community.

Family Violence Prevention Services

7911 Broadway

San Antonio, TX 78209

(210) 930-3669

Web site: http://www.fvps.org

The mission of Family Violence Prevention Services Inc. is to break the cycle of violence and to strengthen families, by providing the necessary tools for self-sufficiency through the delivery of emergency shelter, transitional housing, education, effective parenting education, and early intervention with children and youth.

International Network for the Prevention of Elder Abuse (INPEA)

222 College Street, Suite 106

Toronto, ON MST 3J1

Canada

(416) 978-1716

Web site: http://www.inpea.net

This organization collects and shares information on elder
abuse in an effort to promote education and prevention.

National Coalition Against Domestic Violence

1120 Lincoln Street, Suite 1603

Denver, CO 80203

(303) 839-1852

Web site: http://www.ncadv.org

Organization that works within the community to end domestic violence.

National Domestic Violence Hotline

P.O. Box 161810

Austin, TX 78716

(800) 799-SAFE (7122)

Web site: http://www.ndvh.org

The National Domestic Violence Hotline is a project of the
Texas Council on Family Violence. Help is available to
callers twenty-four hours a day, 365 days a year. Assistance
is available in English and Spanish with access to more than
140 languages through interpreter services.

Violence Prevention Fund (CWF)

Canadian Women's Foundation

133 Richmond Street West, Suite 504

Toronto, ON M5H 2L3

Canada

(416) 365 1444

Web site: http://www.cdnwomen.org

The Canadian Women's Foundation is a national public
foundation that works to improve the lives of women
and girls. There is a section on its Web site with information about violence against women, as well as a list of
programs and resources that deal with the issue.

Web Sites

Due to the changing nature of Internet links, Rosen Publishing
has developed an online list of Web sites related to the subject
of this book. This site is updated regularly. Please use this link
to access the list:

http://www.rosenlinks.com/faq/fam

For Further Reading

Adichie, Chimamanda. *Purple Hibiscus*. Chapel Hill, NC: Algonquin Books of Chapel Hill, 2003.

DeKeseredy, Walter S., and Martin D. Schwartz. *Dangerous Exits: Escaping Abusive Relationships in Rural America*. Piscataway, NJ: Rutgers University Press, 2009.

Evans, Patricia. *The Verbally Abusive Relationship: How to Recognize It and How to Respond*. Avon, MA: Adams Media, 2010.

Feuereisen, Patti, and Caroline Pincus. *Invisible Girls: The Truth About Sexual Abuse—A Book for Teen Girls, Young Women, and Everyone Who Cares About Them*. 2nd ed. Emeryville, CA: Seal Press, 2009.

Goobie, Beth. *Something Girl*. Victoria, BC: Orca Book Publishers, 2005.

Gordon, Sherri Mabry. *Beyond Bruises: The Truth About Teens and Abuse*. Berkeley Heights, NJ: Enslow, 2009.

Johnson, Scott A. *When "I Love You" Turns Violent: Recognizing and Confronting Dangerous Relationships*. Far Hills, NJ: New Horizon Press, 2005.

Levy, Barrie. *In Love and in Danger: A Teen's Guide to Breaking Free of Abusive Relationships*. Emeryville, CA: Seal Press, 2006.

Pelzer, Richard B. *A Teenager's Journey: Overcoming a Childhood of Abuse*. New York, NY: Warner Wellness, 2006.

Index

About the Authors

Vanessa Lynn Michaels is a teacher and writer who lives in California.

Jeremy Harrow lives in Fort Myers, Florida. He has a degree in media and communications and writes books for teens.

Photo Credits

Cover istockphoto/Thinkstock; p. 6 Photodisc/Getty Images; p. 8 © Jim West/ZUMA Press; p. 10 © IndexStock/SuperStock; p. 12 © www.istockphoto.com/Stockphoto4u; p. 15 © AP Images; p. 18 © www.istockphoto.com/ericsphotography; pp. 22, 24, 52 Thinkstock.com; p. 26 © Bob Daemmrich/The Image Works; p. 32 © Jim Varney/Photo Researchers, Inc.; p. 34 Keith Brofsky/Photodisc/Getty Images; p. 37 © David Spencer/Palm Beach Post/ZUMA Press; p. 42 Michael Williamson/The Washington Post/Getty Images; p. 44 © Bryan Patrick/Sacramento Bee/ZUMA Press; p. 46 © The Augusta Chronicle/ZUMA Press; p. 49 © www.istockphoto.com/ Juan Estey.

Designer: Evelyn Horovicz; Editor: Bethany Bryan; Photo Researcher: Amy Feinberg